How to Invest $1 to $1,000 Step-by-Step

The "How it Works" Guide to Building Wealth

By Tiffiny D. Traylor

OTHER BOOKS BY TIFFINY TRAYLOR

Your Best Life: Creating Wealth With What You Have
Today
Publisher: Traylor Books (2019)
ISBN-13: 978-1-7337466-0-1

tiffinytraylor.selz.com
Facebook: Wealth Building Tools
Instagram: @523LifeStyle

Available on Amazon

How to Invest $1 to $1,000 Step-by-Step: The "How it Works" guide to Building Wealth
Copyright © 2020 by Tiffiny Traylor
tiffinytraylor.selz.com
502030LifeStyle@gmail.com

Available on Amazon

~Disclaimer~

I, Tiffiny Traylor, am not a broker/dealer or investment advisor. I have no access to non-public information about publicly traded companies. I cannot be held legally responsible for consequences of financial decisions made as a result of reading this book. I am not regulated by the Financial Services Authority.

I am an educator on analyzing, learning & discussing general information related to stocks, investments and strategies. No content in this book constitutes - or should be understood as constituting - a recommendation to enter into any securities transactions or to engage in any of the investment strategies presented in this book content. I do not provide personalized recommendations or views as to whether a stock or investment approach is suited to the financial needs of a specific individual.

About the Author

My name is Tiffiny Traylor, and I have 15+ years' experience in the finance industry. I am passionate about sharing financial literacy and educating my community on the importance of building wealth. Investing is the ultimate multiplier. The first step is to conquer the challenge of saving money; investing is then your graduation gift. I would love to share with you the simple step-by-step investment strategies that I have implemented to great success. The goal is freedom and it only takes one investment at a time.

Step 1: Save your money. I took several years to save my money, without a specific purpose in mind; I was saving just to save. After ever pay period, I drove to the bank and deposited a specific amount in my savings. Why? Because those numbers made it real, confirming that the amount was increasing. It encouraged me to keep going month after month, giving me a small goal to reach for until I made the next deposit. The original goal was to save eight months' pay for living expenses, or an Emergency Fund. A great stress reliever for sure, but thereafter an asset accumulation which grew by continuous additions and set me up for success in the investment phase.

Step 2: Invest your money. The excitement of investing is very real. Take individual stocks: I like the ups and downs and the ins and out of it all. If my stock is doing well, good. If my stock is down, I will probably buy more at the discount rate and wait for the stock to go up in the future. This is only predicated on the fact that I like the company stock, feel that it will increase in value, and can wait on the return. This has been my strategy and it is working for me!

Then there is the crowdfunding option, the less exciting but just as a promising investment to date. Crowdfunding allows me to invest in a start-up company in their early stages, granting me a greater return when the company is successful. I like seeing a company soar, and my money with it, from the beginner stages all the way through to profit. Patience is necessary here, since businesses do take time to grow; however, the cashflow in the end is well worth it.

Please note, invest responsibly. Make sure you are in a secure financial position before you begin investing. If it were easy, everyone would have money in the bank and a healthy retirement account. Investing requires intention. I purposely save to purposely invest, and I'll teach you to do the same.

Just remember, you are your biggest cheerleader. Celebrate every little win until you reach your ultimate goal. Don't wait for others to cheer for you, you cheer, and let them catch up later!

And remember, sharing is caring. If this book has supplied you with knowledge, confidence and independence please share it with your family and friends.

Yours truly,

Tiffiny Traylor

P.S: If you would like to contact me, I would love to hear from you!

You can reach me at 502030LifeStyle@gmail.com

Dedication

I dedicate this book to my firstborn son, Dequan Fort. You have been my son, my help and my friend, as life reveals. I'm so absolutely proud of the man you are and are becoming. You make me believe that Moms do win. I won when I was blessed to have you. I won every day that I had the pleasure of raising you. And I win now seeing you with a loving family and with children of your own. I look forward to watching you grow and succeed in your goals. I also look forward to our many discussions about money, finance and business. Money talk, that's what "we" do. So very proud of you, SON. Thank you for being YOU.

Introduction

What I wouldn't give to go back to my very first job and have the knowledge I've packed in this book. I know my financial IQ would have been outstanding. But all things have their season. Let's claim this season as Wealth Building FOR YOU. Our lives are so busy and filled with day-to-day tasks. We start the New Year off with determination, then it's Easter and before you know it, it's Thanksgiving…again! How did the year go by so fast? We say that every year, and once again we delay investing in our future.

After reading this book you will:
- Obtain an understanding of investments
- Define what a Portfolio is and what it looks like
- See examples of investments from $1 all the way up to $1,000
- Know the 3 major Income tax rates & how they apply
- Realize which income type has the lowest tax
- Learn what benefits are given to "long term" investments
- Learn a significant dis-advantage to "short term" investments
- Increase your investment IQ
- Build Your Wealth, Plain and Simple!

It is my pleasure to assist you in this journey. Sometimes we just need help focusing on our financial goals. That's where I come in as a friendly guide through the different stages of investing. Here, I have provided you with different investment levels to assist you in generating WEALTH.

Table of Contents

Introduction to Investing

First things first: have you passed the prerequisite that grants you an opportunity to invest? You need three major factors in place before investing: One, are you completely Debt Free? Two, have you saved an Emergency Fund? Three, are you investing in your Retirement Account?

If the answer to all three is YES, pass go. Congratulations, you're ready for the opportunity to invest!

If the answer to any three of the factors are NO, stop now. Go get my book, **Your Best Life: Creating Wealth With What You Have Today"**. Read this book first to get my step-by-step guide to Wealth Building. Take action and prepare for INVESTING later!

With that settled, let's begin investing!

Why do we invest? To gain Income or Cash Flow. What funds do we use to invest? Income from our job or business. The goal is to start with an amount and add to it. No matter what income level you are at currently, that's where you must start investing. Never let the excuse of "I don't make enough money" stop you from investing. Start budgeting with the income you have today. From your budget you will have a clear understanding of what money goes to Expenses/ Savings/ Lifestyle every month. Within your budget you will also allocate funds for investments. Every month, put aside an amount to your Investment Account. Every bit counts towards building a better future for you and your family.

Even $20 a week can generate at least $1,040 per year.

Even $30 a week can generate at least $1,560 per year.

Even $40 a week can generate at least $2,080 per year.

When you build up savings, you will also build your financial confidence. During the time it takes to build an fund, research the types of investments that are of interest to you. Take online courses to educate yourself on all different types of Investments. The key to investing: only invest in the industry you have knowledge of, invest in companies you purchase from and invest in companies you see potential for growth in.

Having a job is great, but having a job and investments are better. If there is a lay-off, you have security because you have investments. If you feel unhappy with your job, you'll be safer because of your investments.

Your job provides one stream of income, while an investment or several investments is a second or third stream of income. The average millionaire has seven streams of income. Depending on a job alone is a losing hand. In order to maximize stability, get stream two or five or seven!

I want to retire early, not at the 65th year of my life. How can you retire early? Only by investing. My goal is to have a net worth large enough to support my lifestyle at age 55. Some suggest to have 25 times their current annual income before retiring. Others say to have enough money to live from the interest yield on the total invested. Or build a successful business and sell it at retirement.

25 Times Income Rule:
Income: $50,000 * 25 = $1,250,000 total to retire
This goal takes both savings and investments to accomplish.

Interest Yield Rule:
Consolidated Investment Total: $1,250,000 * 8% Low Risk Option = $100,000 annual income. At which point you can retire and enjoy life, on your terms. Your $1,250,000 is yours and will stay in your account. The $100,000 is the cash flow that you recycle year after year for life.

What type of an investor are you? There are two categories of investors; non-accredited or accredited.

A non-accredited investor is any investor who does not meet the income or net worth requirements set out by the Securities and Exchange Commission (SEC). Those with an annual income or net worth that is below $100,000 are limited to investing no more than $2,000 or up to 5% of the lesser of their net worth, or annual income. As a non-accredited investor, you'll generally be considered a more inexperienced investor.

To be an accredited investor, you must have an annual income exceeding $200,000, or $300,000 for joint income (married), for the last two years with expectation of earning the same or higher income in the current year. A net worth of $1,000,000 or more will also meet this requirement. As an accredited investor, you'll be considered to be a more experienced investor.

Special note: the taxes on sold stock are higher for short term investing (short term is anything which is less than one year) at approximately 25%. If you purchase stock and then sell that stock within a year, you'll pay that tax.

The taxes for long term investing (long term is anything which is more than one year) are approximately 15%. If your income is lower than $39,375 (or $78,750 for married couples), you'll pay zero in capital gains taxes.

If your income is between $39,376 to $434,550, you'll pay 15% in capital gains taxes. And if your income is $434,551 or more, your capital gains tax rate is 20% (per 2019 tax rate). If you purchase stock and then sell it after one year, you pay 0%, 15% or more.

Capital Gains

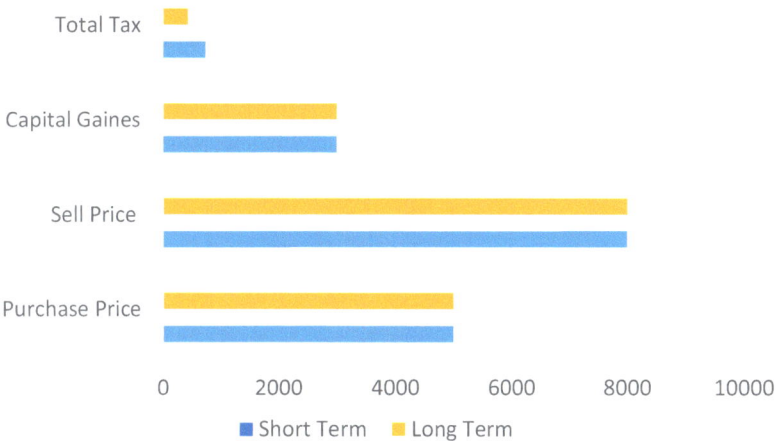

With a $3,000 capital gains income,
your longterm tax payment is $450,
with the short term being $750.
If your income is lower than $39,375 (or $78,750 for married couples), you'll pay zero in capital gains taxes.

The Three Major Stock Markets

Let's take a look at the three largest stock markets to learn where we can start making money:

The New York Stock Exchange (NYSE, nicknamed "The Big Board") is an American stock exchange located at 11 Wall Street in New York City. It is by far the world's largest stock exchange by market capitalization of its listed companies at $30.1 trillion as of February 2018. The NYSE is open from Monday through Friday 9:30 a.m. to 4:00 p.m. EST. The NYSE may occasionally close early, either on a planned or unplanned basis.

The Nasdaq Stock Market (NAHZ-dahk) is an American stock exchange located at One Liberty Plaza in New York City. It is ranked second on the list of stock exchanges by market capitalization of shares traded, right behind the New York Stock Exchange. The exchange platform is owned by Nasdaq, Inc., which also owns the Nasdaq Nordic stock market network and several U.S. stock and option exchanges.

Cboe Global Markets offers trades across a diverse range of products, including options, futures, U.S. and European equities, exchange-traded products (ETPs), global FX, and multi-asset volatility products. Cboe is headquartered in Chicago with a network of domestic and global offices. It is the top listed-options marketplace, the top alternative venue to traditional equity markets, and the first pan-European multilateral trading facility (MTF). It's also the first electronic communication network (ECN) for the institutional foreign exchange (FX) market. These markets have grown to become some of the largest, most-relied upon in the world.

Where is the Money!?
Let's start off clear: there are no instant returns on investments. No one can completely guarantee an investment will make you money (if anyone is trying to, run the other way!). Look at an investment as an **Opportunity for Growth**. No investment going *in* means no Opportunity for Growth coming *out*. Your plan will be to invest in areas that you're knowledgeable in. Whatever interest you, there is an investment stream that will match it. Consider your hobbies and the areas where you're passionate and pursue those income streams.

Additional Benefits to Investing
Paying fewer taxes is what we all want, right? How can you justify a lower tax rate to the IRS? Let's exam the three major taxable options available.

Passive income is earnings derived from a rental property, limited partnership or other enterprise in which a person is not actively involved.

Long-term capital gains (assets held for more than one year) are taxed at three rates: 0%, 15% and 20%, based on your income bracket. For example, a person filing as single, earning less than $39,375, would owe 0% on any long-term capital gains. Advantage!

Portfolio income is income from investments, dividends, interest, and/or capital gains. Royalties received from property held for investment is also considered portfolio income. Portfolio specifically is not earned through regular business activity.
As it relates to dividends, interest, and capital gains resulting from the sale of investments held for longer than twelve months, portfolio income currently taxed at no more than

20%. Furthermore, this income is <u>not</u> subject to Social Security and Medicare taxes. Advantage!

Earned income is obtained by participating in a business or trade. Earned income typically includes wages, salaries, bonuses, commissions and tips.

If your 2019 income is between $43,275 and $88,000 and your filing status is Single, your first $13,500 will be taxed at 10%; every dollar from $13,501 to $43,275 will be taxed at 12%; every dollar from $43,276 to $88,000 will be taxed at 22%; then add Social Security and Medicare taxes on top of that. Total tax will be around 27% of your money. Disadvantage!

Income Tax

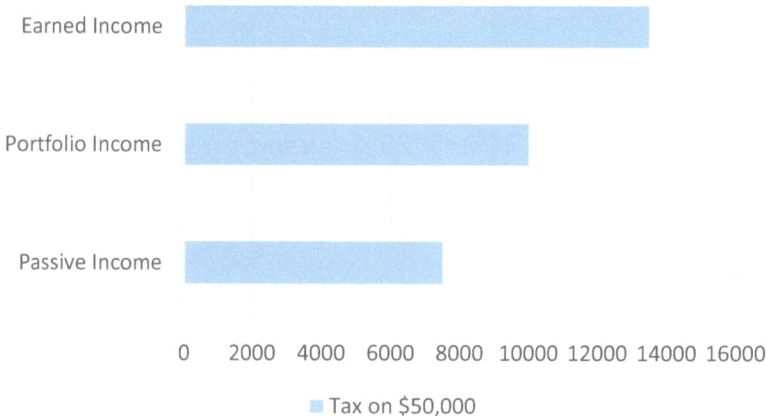

Tax on $50,000

Earned is 27%, Portfolio is 20% and Passive is 15%
The advantage to investing is to pay less tax. As you can see, investing provides the lowest tax available. So go and grow your money!

1099 Tax Form

A 1099 is a record that an entity or person — not your employer — gave or paid you money. The payer usually has to generate the Form 1099 and send copies to you and the IRS. There are several kinds of 1099s depending on the type of income you receive. Why is this a benefit? Your job plus your 1099 income equals your total income, increasing your taxable income and giving you the opportunity to claim tax deductions. However, the best benefit is banking/lender advantages. The best way to get approved for an investment or business loan is income from investments. Adding an additional 5,000 or 10,000 to your regular income is a game changer.

Invest Responsibly

It is up to the individual investor to account for and pay taxes on the profits received from investments each year. I would suggest you set-up a Money Market Saving account to deposit your tax responsibilities into throughout the year. When you submit your annual taxes, the money needed to pay them will automatically be in your savings account.

Example:

Checking Account – Personal Account Only
Savings Account – Personal Account Only
Money Market Saving Account – Tax Account Only

What is a Money Market Saving Account and why is it better than a regular Savings Account? Let's look at this in the (APY) Annual Percentage Yield perspective. When you place your money in a savings account, the bank pays you a rate of about 0.09%. So if you deposit $1,000 they will give you .08 cent a month.

Let's look at the Money Market Savings option. When you put your money in a Money Market Savings account, the bank pays you on average a rate of 1.85%. So if you deposit $1,000 they will give you $1.54 per month.

Please note:
High-risk money market fund holdings can lose value in volatile market conditions or if interest rates drop. Because they are considered investments and not deposits, money market funds are not insured against loss by the FDIC.

Consult the bank of your choosing for the minimum deposit requirements, if any. There could also be withdrawal limits per month that apply.

Portfolio, How it Works (Step-by-Step)

The name of the game is the **Building Up Of Assets**. Your first investment is one step to the beginnings of your Portfolio. Your Portfolio is the range of investments. What does a Portfolio look like?

> Investments:
> 401K Retirement/IRA
> Pension Retirement
> Self-Directed IRA
> Individual Stocks
> Stock Dividends
> Lending Notes
> Crowd Funding
> Business Income
> Real Estate Income
> Mineral Royalties (land)
> Publishing - Intellectual Property

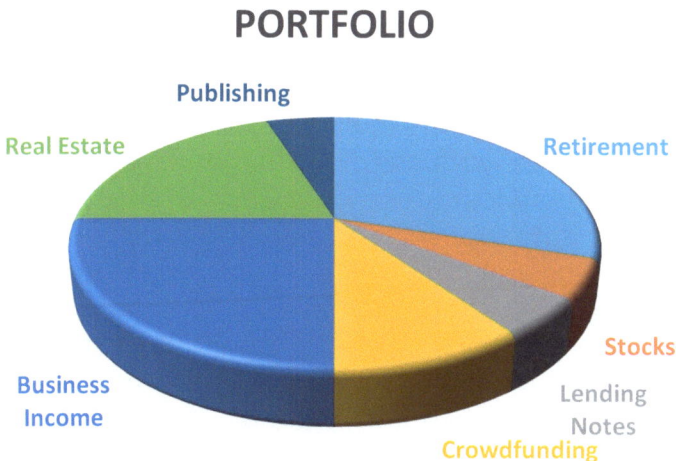

PORTFOLIO

Example. This is to help you understand the many facets of investing on several levels.

You may or may not be interested in perusing all of the options provided. For reference only.

401k Retirement/Roth IRA
Use the company match provided by your employer to fund your retirement. If your company will match 5% to 6% of your salary, dollar for dollar, use that money to fund your retirement with Free Money. This account and IRAs are Tax Deferred; the taxes on this account will not be <u>billed</u> until you retire at 65 years of age.

If you prefer to fund retirement on you own, outside of an employer fund, the Roth IRA is a better option. A Roth IRA is an Individual Retirement Account. This account is funded with After Taxed funds. The taxes on this account will grow tax fee and will <u>not </u>be taxed at age 65.

Pension Retirement
These type of retirement funds are often 100% funded by employers. The funding requirement employees must meet is usually a certain number of years of service; however, the vesting requirement to receive funds from the employer is usually 5 to 7 years for service. Vesting means ownership. This means that each employee will vest, or own, a certain percentage of their account in the plan each year. An employee who is 100% vested in his or her account balance owns 100% of it and the employer cannot forfeit it for any reason. No way to go wrong with Free Money; just make sure to check the vesting requirement before you make any changes to your employment.

Self-Directed IRA
This is the newest and greatest investment opportunity to date. When you end your employment, you have the option to move your 401k account to a self-directed IRA. If you change your job or if you get laid-off, you can take that money in your account and move it into alternative investments. The most popular investment is real estate, such as residential homes, condos, office buildings, foreclosures and even foreign real estate – but an SD IRA also allows you to invest in cryptocurrencies, tax liens, hard-money loans, notes, private companies, hedge funds, startups, IPOs, ICOs, precious metals, foreign currencies, peer-to-peer lending, crowdfunding ventures and much more. Research the companies that are able to manage these funds for you and the fees that are assessed as well.

Special note: money gained from these investments goes back into the fund. With real estate, you can't live in the property you invest in. All monies are held in account until retirement at age 65.

Example:
Take the money from your retirement fund and buy a house for $75,000 cash.

The rental income is $900 x 12 months = $10,800 annual

Your fund will pay all expenses (taxes/ insurance/ maintenance etc.) and the remaining amount goes back into your fund.

You own the property, which increases in value over time, and your fund will have income to invest in other permitted investment opportunities. Building wealth with one investment at a time.

Special note: You have the ability to move a 401k, IRA, Roth IRA and Pension to a Self-Directed IRA. There is also an option to self-manage your funds by creating an LLC in order to own the fund. Please consult a business professional for details.

Example:
Tax Liens. This is simply an easy, passive investment for a gainful return. Property owners that are late paying their taxes are assessed a late fee. You, the investor, pay the property taxes for the current owner when the taxes are late in January. Depending on the date the owner pays their LATE taxes, you the investor gets a return on your money, on an estimate of 6% to 25%.

After several years of non-payment, the county will put the property up for auction. At auction, when the property is sold, you the investor will get your taxes plus interest from the new owner at sale.

Special note: please consult your county of choice for specific details of the interest paid (Tax Liens) and the date the property can be put up for auction (Tax Deeds).

Individual Stocks

Here, you've got tons of freedom: do what you like! Invest in companies that you have most knowledge in for the greatest return. Do you see a positive future for the company? Does the company give a dividend payout monthly or quarterly?

Here's how to calculate the dividend payout:

7.043 Div./ Yield
38.90 Stock Price
2.74 annual pay-out
150 Shares

.07043 x 38.90 = 2.74
2.74/ 4 = .68
.68 x 150 = **$102.74 per quarter.**
That's how much you'll make.

Ordinary dividends earned on your stock holdings are taxed at regular income tax rates, not at capital gains rates. However, "qualified dividends" are taxed at a very advantageous capital gains rate of 0% to a maximum of 15%. For dividends to be classified as "qualified" they must be paid by a U.S. corporation or a qualified foreign corporation and the holding period of the stock must be more than 60 days.

There are plenty of other exceptions and definitions, so check with your broker or tax advisor to see if the dividends for your stock holdings are qualified. Dividends on stock held in a qualified retirement plan are <u>not taxable</u> income.

Lending Notes
Be the Bank! Have you ever thought: "Why can't I get the same interest yield on my money that the banks do?" Now you can! There are several companies on the market that invite you to invest your money to lend it to the general public.

Example:
Start with 60 notes, $25 per note, totaling $1,500.
With re-investing your returns in 6 months, you will have 72 notes.
In 2.5 years you could have 120 notes, PLUS interest!
$120 notes, $25 per note, total $3,000 plus (APY) annual percentage yield.

So with no additional investment, you've doubled your money to $3,000 plus APY.

Crowd Funding

The big score, if you can find a new company in the beginning stages of going public (Pre-IPO). There are several companies on the market now that invite you to invest in companies at the early stages of growth. If you feel the company has potential, you have the opportunity to invest.

Like an angle investor, that initial opportunity is the best opportunity you can get. If you make the right investment that goes from inception to proof of concept, you have a winner. Thereafter to crowdfunding; then to successful business; then to being purchased by a larger company or going public (IPO). That's where you'll see real returns.

The role of crowd funding is to raise funds for the company to research, develop and expand.

The benefits to the investor are:
- equity (ownership) in company, and/or
- Lump sum payout if company is sold, and/or
- Stock discount if the company goes public (IPO)

Business Income

Pick your passion. There so many options available to start a business. You could start an ecommerce, at-home business; transportation, service company etc.

Marketers are offering an Amazon store for $25,000 plus inventory and service fee. The provider will place products for sale, and customers will purchase products. All the expense for inventory is on you while all the profits also belong to you.

An at-home business, like blogging. Create a website, develop a following, and add google cents for advertising. You can blog about whatever you enjoy; like fashion, cars, make-up, finance, robotics, music etc. Take your life's passion to another level with your blog, then use it to make money.

A transportation business, like an independent courier service. A logistics company will hire you to pick-up and deliver goods. Independent couriers own their own vehicles, and have the required insurance needed. You have the option to be the driver or hire a driver. This job usually has a weekly payroll.

A service company, like cell phone repair. This is a terrific business for the mechanically inclined. With training, anyone can start a successful repair business. With very little overhead, you can make a great income from signing up with third party warranty vendors and the general public. If you market your business and do good work, the money will follow.

A service company, like a tax preparer. No one likes doing taxes, and they need to be paid whether the economy is booming or tanking. This is why an at-home tax preparation can be a great business for anyone with a tax background, or anyone willing to take training courses.

Real Estate Income

Tax Liens are a great investment with great returns. By investing in the Property Tax late fees that are due to the county, you'll pay the taxes that are due per the county's list of overdue taxes. When the Property owner pays their taxes, plus interest on late fees, you get paid on returns plus late fees. Start small and re-invest to build a large fund. Then use those returns to re-invest and level up to a larger investment.

Tax Deeds are Properties for sale via public auction per the county provided. The Property for sale could be land only or house & land. Purchasing the Tax Deed includes sales price plus the back taxes owed, per Tax Lien account. You can take possession of the property and sell or rent it, since you'll own it 100%.

Refer to any county Property Tax Office for details for the Tax Lien and the Tax Deed Auctions list and the sale dates. Many counties offer online auctions while some do in person auctions. Refer to the specific county for details and rules.

Royalties (land)

Mineral rights are property rights to exploit an area for the minerals it harbors. Mineral rights can be separate from property ownership. Mineral rights can refer to sedentary minerals below the Earth's crust, or fluid minerals such as oil or natural gas.

The original owner can retain the mineral rights after the sale of property, if written in contract. Subsequent owners can retain rights if they negotiate for them. Know your rights and make sure to have an experienced real estate agent so you're clear on who owns what.

Publishing - Intellectual Property

You can self-publish any content you own in a variety of mediums, such as writing a book, creating courses, music, copywriting and trademarks.

Publishing a book is easy as 1, 2, 3. Once the book is written and proofread, format the book to size and style. You may not know how to do this yourself, so feel free to find freelancers who can help your book look tip-top. Then use Amazon's free publishing platform through Kindle Direct and viola! You're a published author.

To create a course, try using PowerPoint (Microsoft) for free. You can also access companies like Canva and Udmey for more automated applications for a slight fee. After generating a following and need for your content, your digital/paperback product is a GO. Courses are in-demand for many self-help, informational and personal finance fields, and you can sell your products by funneling them through email lists, social media and websites.

Music is the freest form of expression. Create music, upload it to a public platform (e.g. itunes, spotify), and reap the royalties. ACX.com even allows music owners to upload one file to several different platforms at once.

Copywriting is the exclusive legal right given to an originator (you) or an assignee to print, publish, perform, film, or record literary, artistic, or musical material, and to authorize others to do the same. Trademarks are a symbol, word, or words legally registered or established by use as representing a company or product (e.g. the Nike symbol). Your business logo is an trademark and should be protected as such.

Investing with $1

Invest with **Acorns** for $1.   Acorn is an investment app/website that will invest your spare change in a mutual fund (stock).   The stocks are pre-selected depending on your level of investment risk.   There are different investments funds depending on your individual goals.

How it works:
1. Create an account with Acorns app or acorns.com.
2. Link your bank's debt card to your Acorn account.
3. Every time you swipe your debt card, Acorn will round up the spare change to the next $1(e.g. you swipe $20.50/ Acorns will round up $21).
4. Acorn will track the spare change until it reaches a total of $5.
5. Every time spare change reaches $5, Acorn will send that money to your investment fund.
6. Your investment will grow overtime, with no effort on your part at all.
7. Acorn's monthly fee for serving account is $1.

Invest with **Robinhood** for $1. Use Robinhood to acquire single stock investments. This online broker will buy and sell stocks on your behave. There are many companies that offer stocks starting at under $1. Take the time to research and make an informed decision on what to invest in. There is no fee for buying stock, but there is a fee to sell stocks, which is the industry norm.

How it works:
1. Create an account with Robinhood app or robinhood.com
2. Link your bank debt card to Robinhood account.
3. Deposit money in the Robinhood account.
4. Select stocks for purchase.

5. Purchase stocks.
6. Monitor your stocks for gains/ losses
7. Hold your stocks for long term growth (or) Sell your stocks when the identified price meets your goal.

Investing with $5

Invest with **Ebay** for $5. Use Ebay to resell products for profit. Find products at garage sales or around your house to sell on the site. Also, try new items in the clearance section of your favorite store to re-sell. There are millions of people looking for items to buy on this platform (i.e. nation-wide customers).

How it works:
1. Create an account with Ebay app or ebay.com.
2. Create or link your PayPal account for payments.
3. Upload pictures of the products. They're far more likely to be bought with clear photos.
4. List the product with a detail description (brand, size etc.) so people know exactly what you're selling.
5. Sell product.
6. Customers pays to Ebay.
7. You mail the product to the customer.
8. Ebay takes their fee and then forwards the balance to you.

Invest with **Stash** for $5. The company primarily works through fractional shares (a full share split into smaller shares), which allows for you to get in without having huge funds. If it splits up the ownership of a $100 share, you can own a portion of it for $5. Fractional shares allow you to invest in a larger variety of funds, increasing your financial flexibility and portfolio diversification. It also smoothly transitions you into the investment world, rather than forcing you to jump in and buy one high-priced share.

How it works:
1. Create an account with Stash app or stash.com.
2. Link your bank account to your Stash account.
3. Select your investment.

4. Purchase the investment.
5. Monitor the stock for gains/ losses.
6. Hold stock for long term growth (or) Sell stock when the identified price meets your goal.

Investing with $25

Invest in **Prosper** for $25. Proper is a peer-to-peer lending company, which offer returns for lending your money to others. The minimum to open an account with Prosper is $25. The reason for the loan is usually Debt Consolidation, Home Improvement, Personal, Auto etc. You, as the investor, have the ability to review the borrower's credit score, verify their employment, and view their monthly income. An investor commits to loan terms of 36 or 60 months, with an option to sell notes to a third party company if they need to liquidate funds (not guaranteed).

How it works:
1. Create account at prosper.com.
2. Link your bank account to Prosper.
3. Select loan terms of 36 or 60 months.
4. Transfer funds of $25 or more.
5. Add money to account weekly/ bi-weekly/ monthly to build account.
6. Receive monthly payments of principal and interest.
7. Use payments to Reinvest and build up your account (or)
8. Withdraw funds monthly.

Previous Prosper Loans — While I don't exclude new Prosper borrowers, Prosper members who have shown to make timely payments are statistically a much better credit risk.

M1 Finance for $25. M1 Finance as a brokerage also allows you to trade both stocks and ETFs for free. They also let you purchase fractional shares. This means that if Apple stock is currently $400 a share, you can purchase $50 of Apple stock and own 12.5% of a share.

Finally, you can get a free financial analysis from M1 Finance, before you invest a single dollar. As reported, M1 has the largest list of no fee investments available through any brokerage.

How it works:
1. Create account at M1 Finance App or m1finance.com.
2. Connect your bank.
3. Deposit funds in M1 account.
4. Select investments.
5. $0 minimum deposit.
6. Contribute as much as you want to grow your account.

Investing with $100

BlackSeed Capital for $100. BlackSeed Capital is a full service investment company, which also offers an investment club. The BlackSeed Investment Club is a premier investment product which requires a monthly contribution of at least $50. The members contribute monthly to a pool of funds. The club then invests those funds in index funds, individual stocks and ETF's. Each member also has their own personal account through an online investment club portal where they can track their balance and the performance of their portfolio as a whole.

How it works:
1. Download the Voleo app (currently only available via IOS or Android)
2. Submit your email address through the contact form. This allows the club director to send you an invitation through the Voleo app.
3. Once you've received an invite, you must fill out the necessary information to officially join the group.
4. Currently the minimum contribution to start is $100.
5. Monthly contributions are $50+ a month.
6. Website is theblackseedgroup.com

Investing with **Republic** for $100. Republic is a start-up crowdfunding company that offers an array of investment opportunities. Companies available for investment vary from technology and finance to food and social media. Remember that they are all start-ups and you are going to go through the growing challenges of a new business. With this type of investment, you are most safe in investing in several companies and collecting your return as it comes.

How it works:
1. Create account at Republic.co.
2. Select from the list of options to invest in.
3. Enter amount to invest.
4. Fund the investment.
5. Get a return on your investment in 3 ways: when the company makes a profit
6. (or) when the company goes public (IPO)
7. (or) when the company is sold.

Investing with $200

Invest with **Fundanna** for $200. Fundanna is a crowdfunding company that invests in Hemp and Cannabis companies. The money needed to invest will range from $200 all the way up to $1,000. There are several companies that offer options to invest in real estate, growing produce, and RX Networks.

How it works:
1. Create account at fundanna.com.
2. Select investment option to invest in.
3. Enter the amount to invest.
4. Fund your investment with your bank account.
5. Fundanna will verify funds.
6. Fundanna will transfer funds.
7. Fundanna will notify to ownership of investment.
8. The company will communicate updates to investors.
9. Money is locked in until the investment becomes profitable, sold or an IPO.
10. If the company is sold, you get your percentage of ownership, via investment.
11. If the company becomes an IPO, you get stock shares.

Invest with **Amazon** for $200. Amazon has a book reseller market that allows you to make money with used books. The only investment needed is to purchase books, list books on Amazon, and get paid. As a seller you have the option to sell and ship books to customers or send the books to Amazon to process and ship themselves, for a fee. You can find books at garage sales, the Salvation Army, flea markets, recyclers, library sales etc. Remember the whole world over nowadays uses Amazon to buy books: that's a lot for potential customers. Amazon has a catalog of used/ new books with the price they offer. As- long-as you offer a slightly lower price than listed, you should be raking in the sales.

How it works:
1. Create a seller account at Amazon.com.
2. Individual Seller account is free, with a charge of $1 per sale.
3. Professional Seller is $39/ Month.
4. Purchase books.
5. List books on Amazon for sale.
6. Ship book to customer (or)
7. Pay Amazon to process & ship book.
8. Receive Amazon deposit every 2 weeks.

The other way I found books is through online arbitrage. Online arbitrage is a method of buying a book on one marketplace (such as Ebay or Craiglist) to resell on another. Since it's a little more time consuming than scanning or wholesaling, it's best to target books that sell for $25 or more. Textbooks and first edition books are especially great targets.

Investing with $300

Investing with **Constant** for $300. Constant is a peer-to-peer lending company that allows you to lend money to the public for a return. Your investments are fully backed by borrower collateral. You set the amount to invest, you set the APY (9%, 10% etc.), and you set the length of the loan. The length of the loans are one month up to a year. Unmatched portions earn an automatic 5% APY and can be withdrawn anytime. At $300, with 9% APY, your return is $27 annually.

> How it works:
> 1. Create an account at myconstant.com.
> 2. Link your bank account.
> 3. $0 minimum deposit.
> 4. Fund your Constant account.
> 5. Select the APY needed.
> 6. Select the loan length.
> 7. Wait for a Borrow to accept loan agreements.
> 8. Wait for the loan to get accepted.
> 9. Receive your returns.
> 10. If no loans are accepted, receive 5% APY while you wait.

Investing with **Tscer** for $300. The Texas School of Continuing Education and Research is just that, a technical school. There are full scholarships available for the unemployed or disabled. If you need to pay tuition, there is a nominal fee. Here are the certificate programs available: Cloud Security Professional, Cell Phone Repair, Bookkeeping & Accounting, Digital Marketing & SEO, Medical Record and Health Information Technician, and many more.

If you don't live in Texas, look for a technical school in your area for the certificates they offer with full scholarship program.

How it works:
1. Locate and sign-up for class (tscer.org).
2. Compete course.
3. Pass with certificate of completion.
4. Start a Business (or)
5. Get a job.
6. Invest income.
7. Repeat.
8. Build Wealth.

Investing with $500

Investing with **Fundrise** for $500. Fundrise is a crowdfunding company that collects a fund from individuals to purchase real estate properties (commercial and multifamily). Each fund comprises of several projects in several states. You earn returns primarily in two ways: (A) via quarterly dividends and (B) via appreciation in the value of the shares of your investment.

How it works:
1. Create account at fundrise.com.
2. Link your bank account to Fundrise.
3. Select one of three investment plans.
4. Add investment funds to your account.
5. Transfer funds of at least $500.
6. Add money to account monthly to build account.
7. Receive quarterly payments of rental income.
8. Withdraw income.
9. Continue to receive income until property sells.
10. When sold, you will receive final distribution.

Investing with **Tulsa Real Estate Fund** for $500. Tulsa Real Estate is a "real estate"-only   crowdfunding company that purchases property to hold for rental income and to rehab and sell. Another strategy is to also lend money to 3rd parties to rehab their projects with the goal of increasing their investments. If you are looking for an exclusively real estate investment, this might be the one.

How it works:
1. Create an account at invest.tulsarealestatefund.com.
2. Choose investment amount.
3. Fund the account.
4. Monitor investment via online portal.

5. After confirmed funding, you will receive certificate of shares.
6. Please confirm stock and tax certification when received.
7. Return on investment from Rental Income (or)
8. Sale of Property (or)
9. Interest Income from 3rd Part Lending.

Special note: On February 2, 2018, the Tulsa Real Estate Fund ("Tulsa") received its Notice of Qualification as a Regulation A+ Tier 2 crowdfund becoming the first African American owned crowdfunding platform focused on "buying the block."

Investing with $1,000

Investing with **Lending Club** for $1,000. Lending club is a peer-to-peer lending company, which offers returns for lending your money to others. The minimum to open an account with Lending Club is $1,000 and $25 is the minimum requirement to invest in any single note. Your initial $1,000 will purchase 40 notes upon opening an account. You have the option of looking through all notes to see what the borrower is using the money for (e.g. credit cards, moving expenses, car etc.). You can also see their credit score, verify their employment, and their monthly income. Or you can allow the company to select the notes from all grade types and risk levels.

Special note: You have an option to sell notes to a third-party company if you need to liquidate funds (not guaranteed).

How it works:
1. Create account at lendingclub.com.
2. Link your bank account to Lending Club.
3. Transfer funds of at least $1,000.
4. Select loan terms of 36 or 60 months.
5. Build your portfolio. Instead of investing in an entire loan, you can invest in pieces of loans in $25 increments (manual or automated).
6. Receive monthly income of principal and interest.
7. Reinvest or withdraw your funds monthly.

Exclude Loans Already Invested In — Make sure to check this box to make sure you don't invest in the same borrower's note twice. If the borrower defaults on the loan, it will only be one note, not several notes on your account.

Invest with **StartEngine** for $1,000. StartEngine is an equity crowdfunding platform that allows everyday people to invest and own shares in startups and early-stage companies. Founded in 2014, StartEngine is the largest equity crowdfunding platform in the US. Their mission is to help entrepreneurs achieve their dreams by democratizing access to capital.

How it works:
2. Create account at startengine.com.
3. Select investment option of choice.
4. Fund your investment with your bank account.
5. StartEngine will verify funds.
6. StartEngine will transfer funds.
7. Selected company will notify you to investment ownership.
8. Company will communicate with investors for updates.
9. Money is locked in until profitable, sold or made an IPO.
10. If the company is sold you get your percentage of ownership, via investment amount.
11. If the company becomes an IPO, you get stock shares.

The Rule of 72
Now that you have all this money, how can you double your money? The Rule of 72 is a famous shortcut for calculating how long it will take for an investment to double if its growth compounds. Just divide your expected annual rate of return by 72. The result is the number of years it will take to double your investment.

Example: 72 /8% = 9 years
          72 /10% = 7.2 years
          72 /12% = 6 years

Investment of Time and Education.

There comes a time where you will invest in your education and implement the new found information. That time is NOW! Get educated on financial literacy and research it to the fullest.   Find what resources are available: check your local library, acquire a business mentor, go on Google, Youtube etc. Thereafter, take steps to implement the information to reality.   After acquiring the information, you will have the knowledge for life.

Bonus: How to Make $100,000+ a Year

Start a business with the below industries to start on the journey towards financial independence and WEALTH.

Cell Phone Repair Business. Start this business after acquiring the training to obtain financial independence. After you get training (see Invest with $300), sign up to a warranty company (squaretrade.com) as an independent contractor to repair phones and tablets. The average per repair is 30 to 40 dollars. You'll have no expenses, because the company pays for parts and shipping. On top of that, you have the ability to market your services to the general public for additional income. So how will this business make a $100,000 per year?

Warranty company work~
8 phones per day x 5 days a week = 40 phone repaired
$35 per phone x 40 phones = $1,400
1,400 x 50 weeks per yr. = **$70,000** annual income

Your business income~
5 phones per day x 2 days a week = 10 phones repaired
$65 per phone x 10 phones = $650
650 x 50 weeks per yr. = **$32,500** annual income

Total income $102,500

Expense: Training for $1,000

Training School: Google "cell phone repair training".

Please note, expenses are deducted from the $65 per phone income.

There are so many money making options for the cell phone repair business: sell refurbished phones on ebay, social media, buy and flip phones for profit etc.

Appliance Repair Business. Appliance repair is an in demand business, with technicians making $85 per hour on average. A professional training company will train you to repair current products. They will also provide you with warranty companies that contract work to you. You will receive a list of wholesalers for parts. Again, you will have no expenses; the warranty company pays for parts and service fee.   You get paid if the customer pays to complete service or not; it's non-refundable. You also have the ability to market your services to the general public for additional income. So how does this business make a 100,000 per year?

Warranty company work~
4 service calls x 5 day = 20
$85 per hr. x 20 = $1,700
1,700 x 50 weeks per yr. = **$85,000** annual income

Your business income~
1 service call x 5 days = 5
$125 service call x 5 = $625
625 x 50 weeks per yr. = **$31,250** annual income

Total income $116,250

Expense: Training $1,000; insurance (individual cost); parts and transportation (gas).

Training School: Google "appliance repair training".

Share what you've learned! Find a friend or a relative to share this investment information with. If someone has not been exposed to investing and its incredible benefits, let this book be a much needed resource. If the information you've received in these pages has changed your life for the better, pass it on. Change a life and hopefully they will pass it on to the next, keeping the money change going and growing.

Notes

Year 1
Investment Goal for Year 1:
Returns Goal for Year 1:

January 20__
Investment Goal:

Savings:

	Purchase Price	Estimated Returns	Capital Gains	Notes
Investment 1:				
Investment 2:				
Investment 3:				

February 20__

Investment Goal:

Savings:

	Purchase Price	Estimated Returns	Capital Gains	Notes
Investment 1:				
Investment 2:				
Investment 3:				

March 20__

Investment Goal:

Savings:

	Purchase Price	Estimated Returns	Capital Gains	Notes
Investment 1:				
Investment 2:				
Investment 3:				

April 20__

Investment Goal:

Savings:

	Purchase Price	Estimated Returns	Capital Gains	Notes
Investment 1:				
Investment 2:				
Investment 3:				

May 20__

Investment Goal:

Savings:

	Purchase Price	Estimated Returns	Capital Gains	Notes
Investment 1:				
Investment 2:				
Investment 3:				

June 20__

Investment Goal:

Savings:

	Purchase Price	Estimated Returns	Capital Gains	Notes
Investment 1:				
Investment 2:				
Investment 3:				

July 20___

Investment Goal:

Savings:

	Purchase Price	Estimated Returns	Capital Gains	Notes
Investment 1:				
Investment 2:				
Investment 3:				

August 20___

Investment Goal:

Savings:

	Purchase Price	Estimated Returns	Capital Gains	Notes
Investment 1:				
Investment 2:				
Investment 3:				

September 20__

Investment Goal:

Savings:

	Purchase Price	Estimated Returns	Capital Gains	Notes
Investment 1:				
Investment 2:				
Investment 3:				

October 20___

Investment Goal:

Savings:

	Purchase Price	Estimated Returns	Capital Gains	Notes
Investment 1:				
Investment 2:				
Investment 3:				

November 20___

Investment Goal:

Savings:

	Purchase Price	Estimated Returns	Capital Gains	Notes
Investment 1:				
Investment 2:				
Investment 3:				

December 20__

Investment Goal:

Savings:

	Purchase Price	Estimated Returns	Capital Gains	Notes
Investment 1:				
Investment 2:				
Investment 3:				

Year 2
<u>Investment Goal for Year 2:</u>
<u>Returns Goal for Year 2:</u>

January 20__

<u>Investment Goal:</u>

<u>Savings:</u>

	<u>Purchase Price</u>	<u>Estimated Returns</u>	<u>Capital Gains</u>	<u>Notes</u>
<u>Investment 1:</u>				
<u>Investment 2:</u>				
<u>Investment 3:</u>				

February 20___

Investment Goal:

Savings:

	Purchase Price	Estimated Returns	Capital Gains	Notes
Investment 1:				
Investment 2:				
Investment 3:				

March 20__

Investment Goal:

Savings:

	Purchase Price	Estimated Returns	Capital Gains	Notes
Investment 1:				
Investment 2:				
Investment 3:				

April 20__

<u>Investment Goal:</u>

<u>Savings:</u>

	<u>Purchase Price</u>	<u>Estimated Returns</u>	<u>Capital Gains</u>	<u>Notes</u>
<u>Investment 1:</u>				
<u>Investment 2:</u>				
<u>Investment 3:</u>				

May 20__

Investment Goal:

Savings:

	Purchase Price	Estimated Returns	Capital Gains	Notes
Investment 1:				
Investment 2:				
Investment 3:				

June 20__

<u>Investment Goal:</u>

<u>Savings:</u>

	<u>Purchase Price</u>	<u>Estimated Returns</u>	<u>Capital Gains</u>	<u>Notes</u>
<u>Investment 1:</u>				
<u>Investment 2:</u>				
<u>Investment 3:</u>				

July 20__

Investment Goal:

Savings:

	Purchase Price	Estimated Returns	Capital Gains	Notes
Investment 1:				
Investment 2:				
Investment 3:				

August 20__

Investment Goal:

Savings:

	Purchase Price	Estimated Returns	Capital Gains	Notes
Investment 1:				
Investment 2:				
Investment 3:				

September 20__

Investment Goal:

Savings:

	Purchase Price	Estimated Returns	Capital Gains	Notes
Investment 1:				
Investment 2:				
Investment 3:				

October 20__

Investment Goal:

Savings:

	Purchase Price	Estimated Returns	Capital Gains	Notes
Investment 1:				
Investment 2:				
Investment 3:				

November 20__

Investment Goal:

Savings:

	Purchase Price	Estimated Returns	Capital Gains	Notes
Investment 1:				
Investment 2:				
Investment 3:				

December 20__

Investment Goal:

Savings:

	Purchase Price	Estimated Returns	Capital Gains	Notes
Investment 1:				
Investment 2:				
Investment 3:				

Year 3
<u>Investment Goal for Year 3:</u>
<u>Returns Goal for Year 3:</u>

January 20__

<u>Investment Goal:</u>

<u>Savings:</u>

	<u>Purchase Price</u>	<u>Estimated Returns</u>	<u>Capital Gains</u>	<u>Notes</u>
<u>Investment 1:</u>				
<u>Investment 2:</u>				
<u>Investment 3:</u>				

February 20__

Investment Goal:

Savings:

	Purchase Price	Estimated Returns	Capital Gains	Notes
Investment 1:				
Investment 2:				
Investment 3:				

March 20__

<u>Investment Goal:</u>

<u>Savings:</u>

	<u>Purchase Price</u>	<u>Estimated Returns</u>	<u>Capital Gains</u>	<u>Notes</u>
<u>Investment 1:</u>				
<u>Investment 2:</u>				
<u>Investment 3:</u>				

April 20__

Investment Goal:

Savings:

	Purchase Price	Estimated Returns	Capital Gains	Notes
Investment 1:				
Investment 2:				
Investment 3:				

May 20__

Investment Goal:

Savings:

	Purchase Price	Estimated Returns	Capital Gains	Notes
Investment 1:				
Investment 2:				
Investment 3:				

June 20__

<u>Investment Goal:</u>

<u>Savings:</u>

	<u>Purchase Price</u>	<u>Estimated Returns</u>	<u>Capital Gains</u>	<u>Notes</u>
<u>Investment 1:</u>				
<u>Investment 2:</u>				
<u>Investment 3:</u>				

July 20__

Investment Goal:

Savings:

	Purchase Price	Estimated Returns	Capital Gains	Notes
Investment 1:				
Investment 2:				
Investment 3:				

August 20__

Investment Goal:

Savings:

	Purchase Price	Estimated Returns	Capital Gains	Notes
Investment 1:				
Investment 2:				
Investment 3:				

September 20___

Investment Goal:

Savings:

	Purchase Price	Estimated Returns	Capital Gains	Notes
Investment 1:				
Investment 2:				
Investment 3:				

October 20___

Investment Goal:

Savings:

	Purchase Price	Estimated Returns	Capital Gains	Notes
Investment 1:				
Investment 2:				
Investment 3:				

November 20___

Investment Goal:

Savings:

	Purchase Price	Estimated Returns	Capital Gains	Notes
Investment 1:				
Investment 2:				
Investment 3:				

December 20__

Investment Goal:

Savings:

	Purchase Price	Estimated Returns	Capital Gains	Notes
Investment 1:				
Investment 2:				
Investment 3:				

Appendix

Annual Percentage Rate - (APR) is the annual rate charged for borrowing or earned through an investment. APR is expressed as a percentage that represents the actual yearly cost of funds over the term of a loan.

Annual Percentage Yield - (APY) is the real rate of return earned on a savings deposit or investment taking into account the effect of compounding interest. Unlike simple interest, compounding interest is calculated periodically and the amount is immediately added to the balance.

APP - a software application developed specifically for use on small, wireless computing devices, such as smartphones and tablets, rather than desktop or laptop computers.

Capital Gain - a profit from the sale of property or an investment. (e.g. a tax is imposed when individuals part with an asset and make capital gains on it)

Cash Flow - cash flows from investing activities, section on a personal/ company's cash flow statement shows its cash outflows and inflows related to the purchase and sale of investments. The total amount of money being transferred into and out of an account/ business, especially as affecting liquidity.

Collateral - something pledged as security for repayment of a loan, to be forfeited in the event of a default.

Contribution - a gift or payment to a common fund or collection.

(Defined) Contribution Plan - fixed contributions are paid into an individual account by employers and employees. The contributions are then invested, for example in the stock market, and the returns on the investment (which may be positive or negative) are credited to the individual's account

Crowdfund - fund (a project or venture) by raising money from a large number of people who each contribute a relatively small amount, typically via the Internet.

Cryptocurrency - a digital currency in which encryption techniques are used to regulate the generation of units of currency and verify the transfer of funds, operating independently of a central bank.

Debt Free - It means that you do not have to worry about payments or what would happen if you were to lose your job suddenly. It can be revolutionary to think about living debt free. A life without payments is very different from one with payments. Debt free living means saving up for things.

Democratizing - the action of making something accessible to everyone.

Diversification - the action of diversifying something or the fact of becoming more diverse.

Dividend - a sum of money paid regularly (typically quarterly) by a company to its shareholders out of its profits (or reserves).

Exchange Traded Funds (ETF) - an investment fund traded on stock exchanges, much like stocks. An ETF holds assets such as stocks, commodities, or bonds and generally operates with an arbitrage mechanism designed to keep it trading close to its net asset value, although deviations can occasionally occur.

Emergency Fund - a stash of money set aside to cover the financial surprises life throws your way. These unexpected events can be stressful and costly if a fund is not in place.

Equity - the value of the shares issued by a company. The value of a mortgaged property after deduction of charges against it.

Fractional Shares – Less than one full share of equity is called a fractional share. Such shares may be the result of stock splits, dividend reinvestment plans (DRIPs), or similar corporate actions. Typically, fractional shares aren't available from the market, and while they have value to investors, they are also difficult to sell.

Hedge Funds – a limited partnership of investors that uses high risk methods, such as investing with borrowed money, in hopes of realizing large capital gains.

Income Stream - the money a person/ company generates on a regular basis. For example, a company may have a steady income stream from its primary client, and periodic revenue from other, smaller clients. An income stream connotes steady pay.

Initial Coin Offering (ICO) - is the cryptocurrency industry's equivalent to an Initial Public Offering (IPO). ICOs act as a way to raise funds, where a company looking to raise money to create a new coin, app, or service launches an ICO.

Initial Public Offering (IPO) - or stock market launch is a type of public offering in which shares of a company are sold to institutional investors and usually also retail investors. An IPO is underwritten by one or more investment banks, who also arrange for the shares to be listed on one or more stock exchanges.

Interest Yield - the income return on investment. This refers to the interest or dividends received from a security and is usually expressed annually as a percentage based on the investment's cost, its current market value, or its face value.

Mutual Funds - a type of financial vehicle made up of a pool of money collected from many investors to invest in securities like stocks, bonds, money market instruments, and other assets. Mutual funds are operated by professional money managers, who allocate the fund's assets and attempt to produce capital gains or income for the fund's investors.

Net worth - the measure of wealth of an entity, person, or corporation, as well as sectors and countries. Simply, net worth is defined as the difference between assets and liabilities.

Note - Investment promissory note refers to the promissory notes utilized by some individual/ organizations to raise capital for personal/ business purposes. Investment notes are issued by investors in substitute for loan. Investors who invest in a company also take the risk of losing their investment money.

Opportunity cost – represent the benefits an individual, investor or business misses out on when choosing one alternative over another. While financial reports do not show opportunity cost, business owners can use it to make educated decisions when they have multiple options before them.

Pension – a regular payment made during a person's retirement from an investment fund to which that person or their employer has contributed during their working life.

Quarterly – a three-month period on a company's financial calendar that acts as a basis for periodic financial reports and the paying of dividends. A quarter refers to one-fourth of a year and is typically expressed as "Q1" for the first quarter, "Q2" for the second quarter, and so forth.

Rate of Return (RoR) - the net gain or loss on an investment over a specified time period, expressed as a percentage of the investment's initial cost.

Re-invest – put (the profit on a previous investment) back into the same place.

Return on Investment (ROI) - a performance measure used to evaluate the efficiency of an investment or compare the efficiency of a number of different investments. ROI tries to directly measure the amount of return on a particular investment, relative to the investment's cost. To calculate ROI, the benefit (or return) of an investment is divided by the cost of the investment. The result is expressed as a percentage or a ratio. *Example: $500 return/ $200 invest = 2.5% ROI*

Shares – one of the equal parts into which a company's capital is divided, entitling the holder to a proportion of the profits. Represent the equity ownership of a corporation divided up into units, so that multiple people can own a percentage of a business

Startup – a company that is in the first stage of its operations. These companies are often initially bankrolled by their entrepreneurial founders as they attempt to capitalize on developing a product or service for which they believe there is a demand.

Stock – an equity investment that represents part ownership in a corporation and entitles you to part of that corporation's earnings and assets. Common stock gives shareholders voting rights but no guarantee of dividend payments. Preferred stock provides no voting rights but usually guarantees a dividend payment.

Stock Exchange – a market in which securities are bought and sold. The collection of markets and exchanges where regular activities of buying, selling, and issuance of shares of publicly held companies take place. Such financial activities are conducted through institutionalized formal exchanges or over-the-counter (OTC) marketplaces which operate under a defined set of regulations.

Tax Deed – a legal document that grants ownership of a property to a government body when the property owner does not pay the taxes due on the property. A tax deed gives the government the authority to sell the property to collect the delinquent taxes and transfer the property to the purchaser.

Tax Lien – a lien imposed by law upon a property to secure the payment of taxes. A tax lien may be imposed for delinquent taxes owed on real property or personal property, or as a result of failure to pay income taxes or other taxes.

Terms – a fixed or limited period for which something, e.g., office, imprisonment, or investment, lasts or is intended to last.

Third Party - relating to a person or group besides the two primarily involved in a situation.

www.ingramcontent.com/pod-product-compliance
Lightning Source LLC
Chambersburg PA
CBHW041104110426
42740CB00043B/146